SUPER NIFTY CRAFTS

TO MAKE WITH THINGS AROUND THE HOUSE

By Cambria Cohen

Illustrated by Dianne O'Quinn Burke
Photographs by Ann Bogart

Lowell House
Juvenile
Los Angeles

CONTEMPORARY BOOKS
Chicago

NOTE: The numbered stars above the heading of each craft indicate the level of difficulty; one star being the easiest, three stars being the hardest.

Publisher: Jack Artenstein
Vice President, Juvenile Publishing: Elizabeth Amos
Director of Publishing Services: Rena Copperman
Editorial Director: Brenda Pope-Ostrow
Senior Editor: Amy Downing
Art Director: Lisa-Theresa Lenthall
Typesetting and Layout: Michele Lanci-Altomare
Crafts Artist: Charlene Olexiewicz

Lowell House books can be purchased at special discounts when ordered in bulk for premiums and special sales. Contact Department JH at the following address:

Lowell House Juvenile
2029 Century Park East, Suite 3290
Los Angeles, CA 90067

Library of Congress Catalog Card Number is available.
ISBN: 1-56565-361-0
10 9 8 7 6 5 4 3 2 1

CONTENTS

BECOME A MASTER CASTER

WHAT YOU'LL NEED

- newspaper
- water
- large disposable bowl
- 10-pound bag of plaster of Paris (available at hardware or paint stores)
- teacup
- wooden spoon
- petroleum jelly
- wax paper
- white glue
- large bowl
- shallow baking pan
- pliers
- hammer and chisel

DIRECTIONS

1 First, you need to make a mold for your cast. Lay down several sheets of newspaper to catch any plaster drippings.

2 Fill the bowl with one pint of water. Open the bag of plaster. Use the teacup to scoop out the plaster and *slowly* sprinkle it into the bowl of water. The plaster will start to take in the water. *Don't stir yet!* Keep adding scoops of plaster until all the water is absorbed (it should take about eight full teacups). The mixture looks like oatmeal. *Now* stir with the spoon for three minutes. The plaster will begin to thicken.

3 Rub petroleum jelly all over the hand you're going to cast (the hand you do not write with), and place the hand on a large piece of wax paper, palm side down. Have a friend or parent use the teacup to scoop out the plaster mixture and pour it over your hand. Keep your hand pressed flat so no plaster gets underneath.

4 After your hand is completely covered, wait a few minutes until the plaster in the bowl thickens a bit and starts to look like sour cream. Then scoop out enough plaster to make a 1-inch layer on your hand. Now wait three or four more minutes while the plaster dries.

5 When the plaster over your hand starts to feel warm, wiggle your fingers and slowly pull your hand out. The chunk of plaster that is left is your mold! If some of the mold breaks off when you pull out your hand, just glue the pieces back together.

6 Fill the shallow baking pan with water. Turn the mold over so the hand imprint is facing up. Spread the petroleum jelly in the hand imprint, all the way to the fingertips (this will make it easier to chip off the mold later). Place the mold, hand side up, in the pan of water so that only the outside of the mold gets wet. Hold it there for about five minutes. The outside of the mold must be *completely* saturated, or else it will absorb too much water from the fresh batch of plaster that you will pour to make the cast.

7 Take out the mold and lay it on a sheet of wax paper, hand side up. Mix another batch of plaster and, when the plaster starts to get stiff, carefully pour it into the mold, filling the fingertips. Keep pouring the plaster so that it builds up to about 1 inch above the mold to create a base. Let the plaster harden; it will take about twenty-four hours.

8 When you're ready to remove the mold, use the pliers to break off pieces around the edge. Ask an adult to help you use the hammer and chisel to chip away the rest of the mold.

9 Once the mold has been removed, soak the hand cast in soapy water and let it dry. If you need to patch any gouges or chips, just mix a little plaster and water and fill the cracks. You've made a masterpiece—"hands down" !

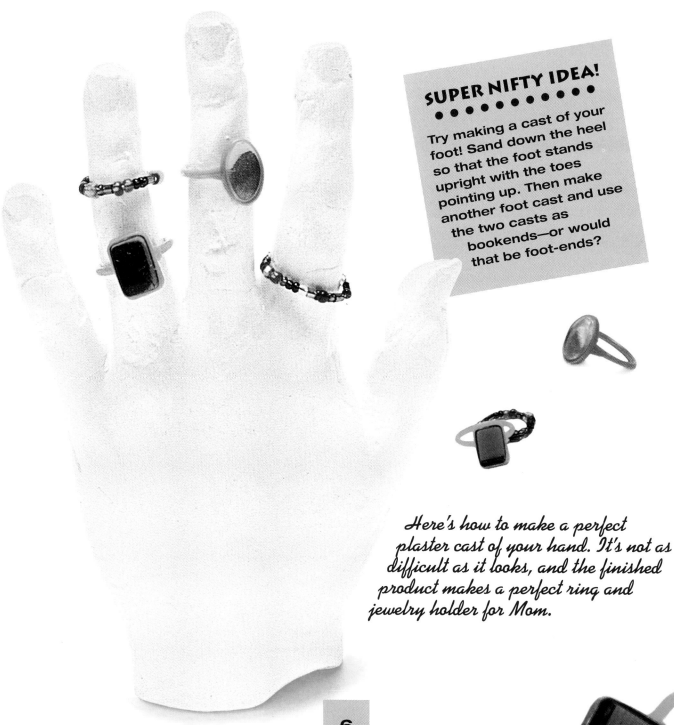

SUPER NIFTY IDEA!
• • • • • • • • • •
Try making a cast of your foot! Sand down the heel so that the foot stands upright with the toes pointing up. Then make another foot cast and use the two casts as bookends—or would that be foot-ends?

Here's how to make a perfect plaster cast of your hand. It's not as difficult as it looks, and the finished product makes a perfect ring and jewelry holder for Mom.

SHAKE IT UP!

WHAT YOU'LL NEED

- empty baby food jar
- small object to fit in baby food jar
- small amount of rubber cement
- water
- teaspoon
- silver glitter
- white glue

DIRECTIONS

1 First clean out the baby food jar. Wash the label off. Hold the small object next to the jar to make sure it will fit inside.

2 Do this next step in a well-ventilated area. Put the lid on a table, upside down so that the inside part is facing up. With an adult's help, put a drop or two of rubber cement in the center of the lid. Stick the object in the cement. Hold the object for a few minutes until the cement hardens. Let the object dry overnight.

3 Now fill the jar with water until the water is about ¼ inch from the top. Put two teaspoons of the glitter in the water for the "snow."

4 Put glue around the inside edge of the lid, and put a few drops of glue around the rim of the jar, too. Screw the lid on. Make sure the jar is upright (the object will be hanging upside down), and let the glue dry.

5 Turn the jar so the object is upright. Shake, shake, shake!

In just a snap, you can create a snazzy snow-dome paperweight like those you see in souvenir shops!

SUPER NIFTY IDEA!

To make a super shaker, use a jelly jar or other large glass jar—then you can glue in larger plastic figures and add twice as much "snow"!

WORKS LIKE A CHARM

WHAT YOU'LL NEED

- small personal objects such as hair clips, buttons, perfume bottles, beads, plastic figures, erasers, rubber animals
- Popsicle® sticks (available at craft stores)
- plastic, silver, or gold charms
- glue
- newspaper

DIRECTIONS

1 To make the frame, glue sixteen Popsicle sticks, edge to edge, into a flat square shape, four on each side. Overlap and glue the inner four sticks at each corner.

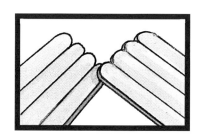

2 Then turn the frame over and glue Popsicle sticks flat, edge to edge, to create a solid back.

3 Now make it charming! Lay the frame on a sheet of newspaper. Glue a charm or object onto the frame. Pick another object and glue it next to the first one.

8

4 Continue gluing objects. Work on alternate sides of the frame so that one side can dry while you're working on another side. Cover as much of the frame as possible.

5 Let the frame dry completely. Then, insert a photograph of the person who will receive the frame. If necessary, trim the photo to fit.

With just a few charms and simple trinkets, this adorable picture frame makes a thoughtful personalized gift for your best friend or a member of your family!

SUPER NIFTY IDEA!
● ● ● ● ● ● ● ● ● ● ●

This picture frame makes a perfect gift for a teacher. Have every student bring an object to glue on the frame, then have someone take a picture of your whole class to put in the frame!

GETTING ANTSY

WHAT YOU'LL NEED

- plastic tub
- soil
- sand
- wooden spoon
- small glass jar (like a jelly or applesauce jar)
- large glass jar (like a peanut butter jar)
- any size jar (to catch ants)
- sugar
- water
- eyedropper
- drinking glass
- stickers
- tempera paints
- paintbrush

DIRECTIONS

1 It's best to do this project outside so that your parents won't have to worry about ants in the house! With a wooden spoon, mix equal parts of the soil and sand in a plastic tub.

2 Take the small jar and place it upside down inside the large jar.

3 Now you've got to catch some ants! Fill the third jar halfway with the soil and sand mixture. Then mix a little sugar and water together in the drinking glass and stir it into the soil and sand. Lay the jar on its side near an anthill or an area where you've seen ants. The ants will be attracted to the sugar.

4 When enough ants have crawled into the jar, pour the ants and soil into the large jar. The mixture will surround the small jar. The narrow field of vision between the large and small jars will give you a good view of the ant tunnels. Add more soil and sand from the tub to fill up the jar.

5 Put the lid tightly on the large jar. You don't need to poke holes in the lid. Personalize your ant farm with stickers and simple painted designs.

6 Watch the ants build their own little colony right inside the jar! Once a week, open the jar and throw in a few bread crumbs or other food scraps. Add some drops of sugar water, too, using the eyedropper.

Design an ant farm that will have all the little neighborhood critters crawling to get in!

MICHAEL'S ANT FARM

SUPER NIFTY IDEA!
• • • • • • • • • •

Instead of ants, why not try pillbugs, earthworms (soil must be kept damp), or any kind of ground beetle? Large glass jars also make great homes for caterpillars, spiders, and other creepy crawlies!

EGG-CEPTIONAL!

WHAT YOU'LL NEED

- egg (one per character)
- large mixing bowl
- needle
- paint
- paintbrush
- scissors
- construction paper
- glue
- felt, fabric scraps, and yarn
- lace or paper doilies
- clear adhesive tape
- any small decorative items, such as flowers, bows, and sequins
- old magazines

DIRECTIONS

1 With an adult's help, blow out the inside of the egg. To do this, first hold an egg over the mixing bowl. Make a tiny hole in one end of the egg with the needle. Then make a hole in the other end, but don't take the needle out. Move the needle around inside the egg till the hole is about 1/2 inch wide. Remove the needle. Keeping the egg over the bowl, blow through the smaller hole. The inside of the egg will come out of the bigger hole. Rinse out the egg with cool water and gently dry it off. Repeat if necessary.

2 Paint the egg. While the egg is drying, make a stand for your egg by cutting a strip of construction paper about 4 inches long and 1 inch high. Decorate your stand by drawing flowers, stars, or even a tie and collar. Then glue the two ends together and set it aside to dry.

 Once your egg is completely dry, you can give your egghead some personality! Cut out felt or construction paper to make eyes and a nose. Or thumb through an old magazine and cut out goofy-looking facial features. Use the markers to add details. Draw on a mustache, freckles, or a goatee! For hair, glue on strands of colored yarn.

4 To make a hat, cut a circle out of light cardboard or construction paper. Turn it into a cone shape by cutting a narrow triangle out of the circle and bringing the edges together, slightly overlapping them. Glue or tape them together. Decorate the hat however you wish.

SUPER NIFTY IDEA!
• • • • • • • • • •

When you blow out the inside of your egg, don't let it go to waste. Give it to Mom and ask her to whip you up a chocolate cake or a vanilla custard cream pie!

These little egg people are so much fun to make, you'll want to create your own eggs-clusive population!

MAGIC MOSAIC

WHAT YOU'LL NEED

- large piece of cardboard, 2 feet square
- pencil
- glue
- toothpicks
- small, colorful, textured items such as broken eggshells, macaroni, rice, dried beans, dried peas, seashells, blades of grass, dried flowers, popcorn kernels, leaves, walnut shells, sunflower seeds, sequins, beads, and cut-up drinking straws
- scissors
- string

DIRECTIONS

1 On the cardboard, draw a big picture using the pencil. This will be the outline for your mosaic. It can be a scene, an animal, a self-portrait—whatever you want.

2 Use dabs of glue to fasten toothpicks onto your pencil lines. You may need to bend or break the toothpicks for the short and curved lines.

3 Pick one item, such as sunflower seeds, and fill one section by gluing them down. Try to fill the entire space so no cardboard shows through.

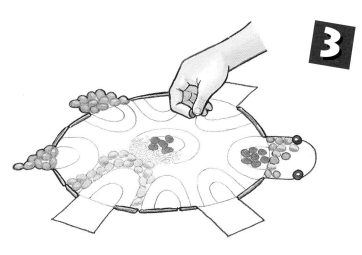

Now choose another item, one with a different color and texture, and fill the section next to the one you just filled. Repeat until all the sections are covered. It should look like a patchwork quilt. Let your mosaic dry overnight, then shake it gently to get rid of any loose pieces.

 With an adult's help, use scissors to punch a hole in the two top corners of the cardboard. Thread a 2½-foot piece of string through one hole and out the other hole. Bring the two ends together in the back of the mosaic, and tie a knot. Now your mosaic is ready to hang.

SUPER NIFTY IDEA!
● ● ● ● ● ● ● ● ● ● ●

If you like this craft—think BIG! Talk to your teacher at school about creating a gigantic, wall-sized picture with the help of everyone in your grade. Now, that's an A+ project with a lot of *class*!

See how everyday items take on a whole new meaning when you mix them in a mosaic!

FAN-TASTIC!

WHAT YOU'LL NEED

- about twenty Popsicle® sticks (available at craft stores)
- light cardboard
- crayons, markers, or tempera paints, various colors
- masking tape
- pencil
- scissors
- glue

DIRECTIONS

1 First, cut the cardboard to make the front and back pieces of your fan. They should be the same size and shape, and the shape can be anything you want. The fan should be about 9 inches wide. Cut out a semicircle from the bottom of each piece.

2 Draw a design on one side of the front piece. Do the same with the back piece.

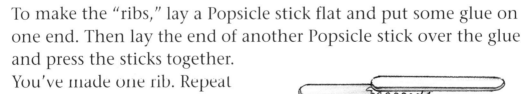

3 To make the "ribs," lay a Popsicle stick flat and put some glue on one end. Then lay the end of another Popsicle stick over the glue and press the sticks together. You've made one rib. Repeat until you have three ribs.

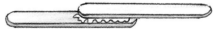

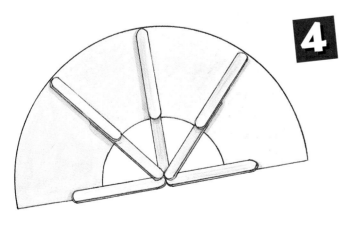

4 Lay the front piece of your fan flat, colored side down. Glue the ribs onto the plain side, bringing the three ends together to form a point as shown. Then glue one Popsicle stick to each corner, bringing their ends to a point as well. Let the glue dry.

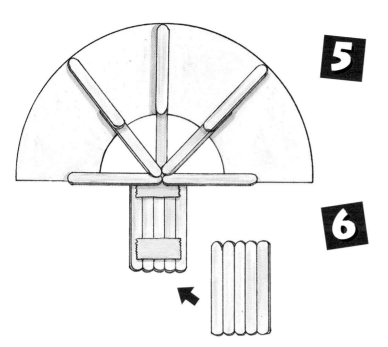

5 Pick up the back piece of the fan and glue it onto the front piece, matching up the edges. The two plain sides should be facing each other. Let the glue dry.

6 Next, make the handle by laying five Popsicle sticks flat. Put a piece of masking tape across the top and the bottom. This is one half of your handle. Glue it to the base of the fan.

7 Repeat using five more sticks and two more strips of tape. Take the second handle and glue it on the other side, aligning it with the first handle. Decorate the handle in all the colors of the rainbow!

SUPER NIFTY IDEA!

These fans make great party favors at any summer birthday or barbecue. Be sure to write the date of the party on the fan for a keepsake every guest will love!

This handmade fan is perfect for a hot summer day!

IT'S AN ORNAMENTAL MELTDOWN!

WHAT YOU'LL NEED

- 3- or 4-quart saucepan
- plastic berry basket
- kitchen tongs
- aluminum pie pan
- small glass beads

- any plastic-coated wire (available at hardware stores)
- scissors
- glue
- glitter

DIRECTIONS

1 With an adult's help, fill the saucepan with water and heat it on the stove (but don't boil it). The water should be deep enough to completely cover the basket.

2 With an adult's help, drop the plastic basket into the hot water. When the basket has collapsed and changed shape, have an adult pull it out using the tongs. Put it on a pie pan to cool.

3 Now string some glass beads onto a 24-inch piece of coated wire. *Make sure to cut off any wire ends that are showing.* Weave the beaded wire in and out of the holes in the basket. The wire will conform to the shape of the basket.

4 Put dabs of glue on various areas of the basket and sprinkle glitter over it.

5 To make a hanger, cut another piece of coated wire about 5 inches long. Weave it through one of the holes. Tie both ends together at the top.

SUPER NIFTY IDEA!
• • • • • • • • •

Try dropping a plastic cup into the hot water. It will melt into a holiday bell shape. Use colored cups for variety. To make a hole for hanging, ask a parent to help you poke a hole in the top with the end of an unbent paper clip.

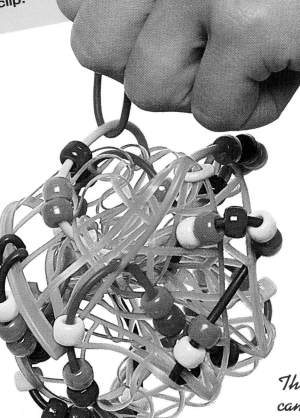

This nifty ornament can be made right in your own kitchen!

A REALLY BIG SHOE

WHAT YOU'LL NEED

- newspaper
- big, old shoe (canvas works best, but leather is fine, too)
- full-strength starch
- water
- small pie tin
- wide paintbrush
- thin paintbrush
- tempera paints, various colors
- small indoor or outdoor potted plant that fits inside the shoe

DIRECTIONS

1 Before you begin, lay down some sheets of newspaper on your work table.

2 Now put the shoe on the newspaper. If there are any shoelaces, remove them. To papier-mâché the entire shoe, first tear up several thin strips of newspaper and set aside. Mix $2/3$ cup of starch and $1/3$ cup of water in a pie tin. With a wide paintbrush, paint the starch mixture all over the shoe.

3 Then, dip a newspaper strip completely into the starch and pull out the strip while wringing it between your fingers. Apply the strip to the shoe, and continue until the whole shoe is covered with newspaper strips. Do two layers of papier-mâché, allowing the first layer to dry before you apply the next. Let the papier-mâchéd shoe dry overnight.

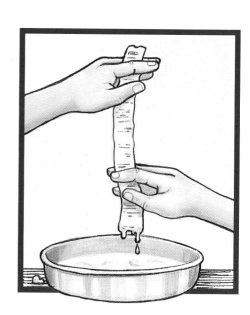

4 Once the shoe is stiff and dry, paint it! Be creative. With the thin paintbrush, make lightning bolts, symbols, or fake buckles and laces. Let the paint dry overnight.

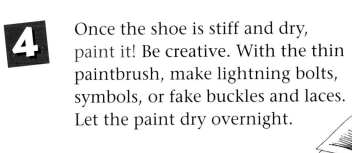

5 Now, *leaving the plant in its original pot,* place it inside the shoe. Keep your craft in the sunshine, and don't forget to water it—the plant, *not* the shoe!

Take a "step" in the right direction by turning an old shoe into a playful planter!

SUPER NIFTY IDEA!
• • • • • •
Try this nifty craft again using a different kind of shoe—maybe an old high-top or penny loafer!

A ROSE IS A ROSE

WHAT YOU'LL NEED

- red and green tissue paper
- cup or bowl
- scissors
- wire stems (available at florist's shops)
- stapler
- florist's tape (available at florist's shops)
- pencil

DIRECTIONS

1 First, cut eighteen squares of red tissue paper. Each square should be about 4 inches by 4 inches.

2 Next, put the cup or small bowl upside down on a stack of about four tissues and trace around it with the pencil. Cut out the circles. Repeat with another stack until you have eighteen circles.

3 Then make a small loop at one end of a wire stem. Thread six circles onto the stem, by poking the pointed end through the center of each circle. Bunch the circles loosely around the loop, then staple them once at the bottom.

4 Do the same with six more circles and staple them onto the others. Then repeat with the last six circles.

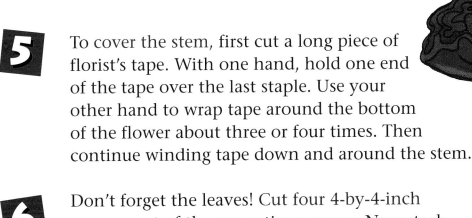

5 To cover the stem, first cut a long piece of florist's tape. With one hand, hold one end of the tape over the last staple. Use your other hand to wrap tape around the bottom of the flower about three or four times. Then continue winding tape down and around the stem.

6 Don't forget the leaves! Cut four 4-by-4-inch squares out of the green tissue paper. Now stack them and cut out a three-leaf shape. With the florist's tape, tape the leaves onto the wire.

7 Finally, fluff out the rose layer by layer so it looks like it's in bloom.

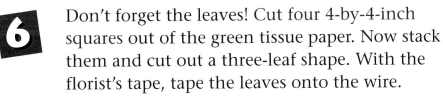

SUPER NIFTY IDEA!

Combine this craft with the Walking on Eggshells bottle vase on page 28. Now, *that's* super nifty!

Even a paper rose, by any other name, is still a beautiful rose.

MAKE A GOOD IMPRESSION

WHAT YOU'LL NEED

- apples, potatoes, mushrooms
- kitchen knife
- several sponges
- scissors
- several empty milk cartons
- tempera paints, various colors
- computer paper
- two wooden dowels, at least 1 inch wider than the computer paper
- glue
- string

DIRECTIONS

 First, prepare your printing tools. With an adult's help, slice a raw potato in half and carve a heart on the inside of one half. Then dig out the potato around the heart so that the heart sticks up. Leave the other half uncut. Do the same with the apples and mushrooms, except cut different shapes. With scissors, cut some of the sponges into squares, circles, and triangles.

 To make a stamp pad, cut a clean milk carton to about 3 inches high. Cut a sponge to fit in the bottom of the carton, moisten it with water, and pour some paint on it. Do the same with another milk carton and a different color of paint.

3 Spread out several sheets of computer paper, but don't tear them apart.

4 Now go stamp crazy! Choose a printing tool, dip it in your stamp pad, and stamp it all over the paper. Repeat with a different tool (anything that will make an interesting shape or texture) and a different color. Make sure you have plenty of objects, because each can probably be used with only one color.

5 To add the finishing touches, tear your artwork off at the top and bottom and let it dry. Then put glue on a wooden dowel and roll the top sheet around it twice. Take the second dowel and do the same with the bottom sheet.

6 Cut a piece of string about 2 feet long. Tie each end to opposite ends of the top dowel. Now your artwork is ready to hang!

Did you know that you can create interesting textures and patterns using simple household objects—including fruits and vegetables?

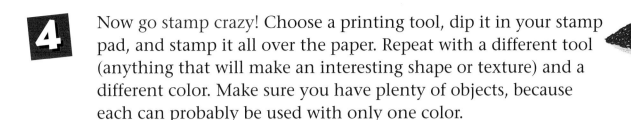

SUPER NIFTY IDEA!
• • • • • • • • •

When you make this wall hanging, use light-colored paints. Then, in a dark bright color like purple, paint a large "Welcome Friends" in the center. Hang it on your bedroom door. What a way to make a good impression on visitors!

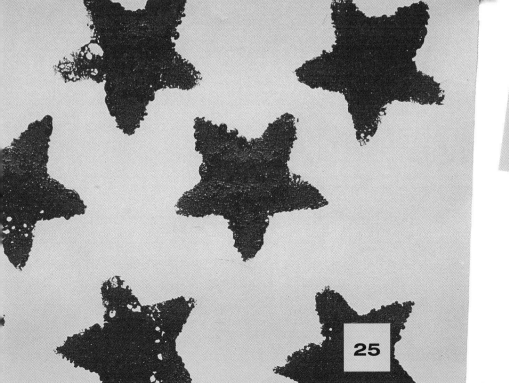

25

THE BEST BIRTHDAY BOX

WHAT YOU'LL NEED

- **two sheets of square origami paper (or gift wrapping paper)**
- **puff paints or markers**

- **scissors**
- **cotton balls or tissue paper**
- **ribbon**

DIRECTIONS

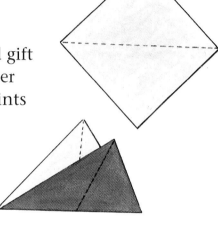

 For this project, if you're not using preprinted gift wrapping paper, it's easier to decorate the paper before you fold the form. You can use puff paints or markers to draw fun designs, such as tiny candles, stars, polka dots, or flowers.
Then, with your paper in a diagonal shape, colored side down, fold the bottom point to the top point, then the left point to the right point, crease it firmly, then unfold.

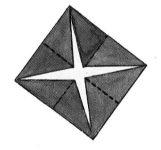 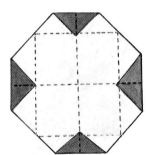

 Now fold each point to the center, then unfold.

 Fold each point to the crease lines that you just made, then unfold.

 This next step is a little tricky. Take the bottom point and fold it so it reaches the second crease line from the top point, then unfold it. Then take the top point and fold it down so that it reaches the second crease line from the bottom point. Unfold it. Repeat this step on the two sides, then lay your form flat.

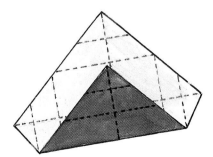

26

5 Using scissors, cut along the lines, as shown in the illustration.

6 Fold in the top and bottom points so that they meet in the center of what will be the bottom of the box. Bend in the ends of the two sides to form a box.

7 Fold the left and right sides up and into the box so that the corners meet in the middle. That's the bottom half of your box.

8 To make a lid, repeat steps 1 through 7 using a piece of paper that is ¼ inch larger than what you used for the bottom of the box.

9 Tear apart several cotton balls or get a few small pieces of tissue paper to line your box, then fill it with a small gift such as earrings, a bracelet, or candy. Put the lid on, then just tie it with the ribbon to give a gift that will be treasured forever.

Celebrate today by making a sturdy gift box to fill with treasures for friends and family on their birthday!

SUPER NIFTY IDEA!

Glue four boxes together—bottoms only—in a row or in a square shape to create your own desk organizer. Use each box to hold small items such as rubber bands, paper clips, thumbtacks, and knickknacks!

WALKING ON EGGSHELLS

WHAT YOU'LL NEED

- dozen raw eggs
- large mixing bowl
- glass bottle, shoe box, or tin can
- newspaper
- tempera paints, various colors
- tacky craft glue
- paintbrush

DIRECTIONS

 Break twelve eggs in half, then carefully rinse out each egg half with cool water. (Don't throw the insides away—cook them for breakfast!) Allow them to dry for 30 to 60 minutes.

 Spread out a few sheets of newspaper and put the empty shells on top. Cover them with another sheet of newspaper. Now get your shoes on and stomp all over the shells to crush them. The shells should be in tiny pieces, not powder. When you're through, take off the top sheet of newspaper.

3 Put glue all over the bottle, shoe box, or can. Then roll it in the crushed eggshells, making sure it gets completely covered. If needed, add extra glue to those spots where the shells are not sticking. Let the glue dry.

4 Finally, use the tempera paints to color the eggshells. Make stripes, polka dots, zig-zag patterns . . . anything you can imagine!

Did you know you can dress up bottles, boxes, and cans with crushed eggshells?
It's eggs-traordinary!

SUPER NIFTY IDEA!

What other foods have shells that lend themselves to being crushed and painted? How about peanuts? You'll have as much fun eating the yummy nuts as you will creating a nutty shell vase or box. Just shell the nuts and follow the directions above.

BAG IT!

WHAT YOU'LL NEED

- old pair of blue jeans
- needle and thread
- heavy scissors

- Velcro™
- buttons, fabric patches
- puff paints

DIRECTIONS

 Start by cutting off the legs of the jeans about an inch below the fly. Save the legs to make into a strap.

2 If you've never sewn before, ask a parent or older brother or sister to help you out. Cut a long piece of thread about the length of your arms outspread. Then thread it through the needle and tie a knot.

3 Bring together the front and back of the jeans legs at the bottom and sew them closed. Make small, tight stitches. You should go back and forth over your stitches at least twice to reinforce the bottom.

 Next, you'll need to make a clasp to hold the top of the bag closed. Get a piece of Velcro at least 2 inches long. Sew one half to one side and the other half to the other side. When you close the bag, the two Velcro pieces should align.

5 To make the strap, take one pants leg and cut it in half the long way. Take one half and fold it in half lengthwise, then sew the pants leg closed.

6 Now sew each end of the strap to the sides, inside the waistline. Sew the strap securely, otherwise it may break when your bag is full.

7 Decorate your bag with buttons, fabric patches, and puff paints. Now you're a real blue-jean baby!

SUPER NIFTY IDEA!
● ● ● ● ● ● ● ● ● ● ●

Make a matching money purse with your little brother's or sister's pair of jeans. (Be sure to get a parent's permission before taking them!) Or, if you want a *really* small coin container, find jeans made for a doll and sew away!

Here's how to turn an old pair of blue jeans into a cool-looking purse, gym bag, or beach bag!

USING YOUR NOODLE

WHAT YOU'LL NEED

- string or heavy thread
- scissors
- newspaper
- craft paints, various colors
- paintbrush

- an assortment of dried pasta with holes, such as macaroni, wagon wheels, mostaccioli, and rigatoni

DIRECTIONS

1 First, figure out how long you'd like your piece of jewelry to be. Then measure the string around your neck, wrist, or ankle.

2 Lay out newspaper to cover your work area. Use craft paints to paint the pasta all different colors before you string them. Allow them to dry for an hour.

3 Start threading the pasta shapes in any order you like. When you're done, tie the two ends of the string into a big knot. Give them as special gifts to your friends and family.

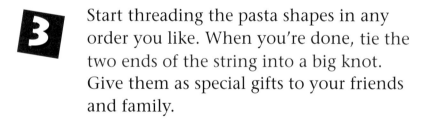

SUPER NIFTY IDEA!

Mix in other colorful objects with the pasta shapes, such as buttons and various sizes of beads, both plastic and glass. These add nice variety to your pasta jewelry.

Here's a nifty way to "pasta" time— making cool, colorful jewelry out of all those great macaroni and pasta shapes!

DATE DUE

DEMCO